The Northern Biochemist

J A Elcock

This is book **76** of 100 copies

First published in 2013
The Artel Press

Copyright © J A Elcock, 2013

ISBN 978-0-9926035-0-2

Printed in the UK by Imprint

Heather, for allowing this to happen.

CONTENTS

Höfuðborg hins bjarta Norðurs

Здесь будет город заложен
На зло надменному соседу

Deus nobis haec otia fecit

AKUREYRI

Island inlet. Approach gently, dissolve
your Western preoccupations in the Iambic
brine, a sinewy, silky trail whose
birth is tantalisingly, truly, due North.

Step quietly. O far Faroese gut and
Aeolic gene, yet still the grey translucent
warmth kindles your northern climate within.

Head forth. Bravely now the oars bend the
bruising wind, fulmar's friend and foreign foe.

Rest now. Would you feign foreigner?
Live a lie of quiet suburban shores in
these subarctic moors?

Head then. Homewards, southbound, cross-grain,
willow-beaten, egged on by cathartic climes, you
Gallic Saxon Swine, you
artisan - go seek thy soul up t'North.

BIRD POEM

Nestled in two cupped hands
and weightless, lay you.
Innocent and hollow-boned,
frenetic in your heartfelt quivering;
less urgency, no fear.
Rather, an unfamiliarity with
being bed-bound and land-locked.

Little bird, I have rooted you
earthen-like to my clumsy hands.
Pegged you, as a tree to mistletoe,
earthed your vital spark, the very thing
that keeps you aloft.

So go now, little heart, spirit of God. Go soft.

MIRRORED

Could Yorkshire stone beaten,
cut, enslaved and bound in that
ley 'tween two pillars reflect as
much as glass, viewed dimly 'midst
the autumn gloam?

Elsewhere a mirror hangs, whose honest
frame once hid in forests far,
traded light for the gloom of
a foreign hold and foreign hands,
to embrace the silvered glass whose
crazed surface could speak of much.

For two hundred years of shuffle,
step, sidewalk and sloth do much
in their turn to trade earth with sky.
Grit, more hard than glass!
Sweat-laden, green-gray Georgian stone.
October street, shoe-shodden street of Hope.

TRANSVERSE SECTION

Supine and pinned gently to the steel slate against an oily film,
the waxy flesh pulls tenderly to the day bed.

Would the knife pare down, circumnavigate an exploring mind
and empty belly, leach yearning, bleed learning.

Collect the spoils drop-like on a slidecover for future exploration
- for what it's worth!

In the full-light, hertz-laden glare of the coldroom,
that's the place to test a journey's worth.

Scrutinise this - write me a novella with ink from a blood group,
paint me a picture through glazes of an haematocrit.

In a divided self, microtomed for public view or private consumption
I am at last dispersed and conquered. Turn off the light.

CENTRAL STATION

The crown of the hill splits open,
riven from within, breaking the levy.
See the liquifying moraine of fire
laying the bride bare,
cauterising her wound.
Living, luminescent flame curls the chasm,
a new Exchange of sulphurous light
where once coke plied its tracks.
Verso, the ragged embankments
tumbling to the sea, where
bemused citizens cast whimsical glances.
Purge your way Bold river,
into a light, fantastic trip from perdition.
For sepulchral now stands the cooling buildings,
headstones for a city in transition.

ROMAN ROAD

I'm just going down to the Dell. Past
the glass-strewn playground, 'neath the stables,
drawn close to the Old Hall, picking a track
cleft to the old Course. Past loves, past lives.

I'm just going down to the Dell. Warm
fog of chatter, chinks of drinks, clatter
of glasses. To pull together well-worn,
copper-topped tables. To listen, to love.

I'm just going down to the Dell. Secret
way, Roman Road, carved and craven winding
way of nettle and bottle. Connecting
somewhere, to nowhere.

Let me show you the way there. Delve
deep on the green track, hop the worn stones that
roam. No leather-shod Legion,
just a happy misnomer. Alone.

вчера - сегодна

A sky pinned north for
Billowing drapes of translucent
Cloud to belly-down in a
Lilac glaze towards a
Wintry town.

The gap withal poised to
Discharge its quilted load -
More anticipation than
Trepidation; a beautiful,
Pregnant, appropriate, pause.

———

The paves smeared with a
Dirty marmalade of ice, a
True hangover from the
Night's vitruvian excesses.

A sky unloaded, hoisted high and
Wet with light, a blue-bounded
Parasol of watercolour
Painted in post-coital joy,
Released from Russia's icy grasp.

ANNA

Lead me into the garden.
Hold my hand and turn me. Let me whisper.
Let me smile at your blowzy, elfish wonder,
Regard the gracious dip of your chin.
Your eyes, scooped, scallops of pure green
Oyster-like loveliness.

My third rib, Anna. My oneness
Wonder-girl, life-giving, gentle beauty.
Grace, abounding. Kindness, embodied.
Your spirit runs ever-childlike, a
Pure rivulet of golden goodness
Bringing light and life to all.
Sweetheart, lock-curling grin. Anna.

WHEN GOD VISITED CHELYABINSK

Drumming fingers idly stroking the dash
count down the lights, in the thinness of a
Siberian dawn.

Hissing steam of the egg pan, greasy fingers
clear a view to glimpse the usual day.
Bumping pushchairs negotiate empty playgrounds,
frosted and huddled desert-like in the grey.

Multitudinous minor moments of whimsical
windswept existence in the Urals,
the dailiness of life viewed through the panes. A
melancholic vista, filtered so unexpressingly through
the dystopian stage set of a Soviet planner.

Somewhere, a dead leaf fell, a clock ticked
and the wheels of a trolleybus gently squealed.

And Lo. There, arising in the East
stood Gabriel; unfurling white wings
flowered - bloomed in a Glory of
prophetic majesty.

His sword stretched, rent the sky
in a persuasive, unrelenting violence.
The very blue - transfigured,
an unbroken stream of light distilled itself
growing in an unbridled intensity.

If the finger of Christ himself had dipped
the firmament, the burst of light that
breached the void would not give justice
to this unfolding flame.

Fuelled from the sap of the tundra,
potentiated by the pure Northern air, such was
His arrival. The light yet a mere
Lenten candle - hear now the altar bell!

Ten thousand seraphic voices acclaiming as one
воскресение - He is risen indeed.
A logarithmic burst of sound rebounded
around the town, immutable and unworldly,
the clamour of the herald angels.

Why little Chelyabinsk? Holy place, mother country,
sacred space? What passes now with privilege?
Rare expectation, prescient for these
triffid-touched with an uncertain yet blessed future.
Chelyabinsk, anointed by a chasm of light.

Somewhere a clock stopped. The lights changed.

AT THE FOOT OF THE STAIRS

At that moment, at the foot of the stairs.
Where hearts leapt,
Where unrequited thanks caught you
Poised, teetering between the ages.

For elegiac, confident, distillation of youth.
For bluff and beauty, for wisdom - forever.
Deep knowledge, deeper self-divided intent.
Still the stairs find you reaching and wanting.

This natural, correct and wondrous place;
Reminded at this point, at the foot of the stairs.

Longer time, time spent then and now, forgotten
but will grow again. Take your time. Poised. I will pause.

VIEW FROM NOVA SCOTIA

Leaning into abstraction,
Literally, leaning. Peering
Through 45° plane, vertical;
Yet inclined, to decline
The superficial, and
Embrace still, the corporeal,
Yet intangible - without.

петроградъ

City of rude birth, delivered on Karelian marshes
by the labour pains of two hundred thousand souls.

A Caliban conception, mired in the sloes
and blackfly, foretold dimly in the thin
light of a winter sun.

Christ-like resurrection clad in
white robes of marble and living veins of the Neva;
land liberated from its feudal wilderness.

In dying you destroyed my death,
glittering domes where clay and standing water was.
Lignified in the cruel mantra: Rodina.. Mother.. God..

Blood spilled, sky pierced. Streets crucified
and pock-marked by shrapnel, instantly redeemed
by the golden hypodermic of the Admiralty.

Soul discharged, boil lanced. Healing power
of this hero city. Granite-blooded
amber touchstone of the Baltic.

DENMARK STRAIT

White-lipped, dread meniscus.
Immutable boiling void.
Threatening, quietly mocking
our paltry flame.

Thirty three degrees of separation.
Insatiable mouth.
Idly waiting to snuff out heat,
Absorb goodness, badness...

Strange then how gulls are welcomed -
such benign ambivalence.
Seeking the company of fowl,
lost as it is to our comprehension.

Cerulean slab,
Weighted by an ageless sobriety.
Grey light, flames of wind,
horizon-less terroir of fear and emptiness.

Welcome us,
into your life-giving, sepulchral calm
of liquid ink beneath. A richer vintage
for that last, lung-expiating kiss.

66°

Gentle moment.
Broad waters.
Northern diver.
Glacial grace.
Divine momentum.
Wonder valley.
Point of motion.

HIRUNDINIDAE

Can you draw the line, describe the bind
Tying you both together?
Trace the route that has paired your lives?
For flecks in our plumage mark something of the self,
Yet observe the sgraffito on the egg, etched by many hands.

Gaze in the mirror, see your soul lies locked,
Trapped in flesh as the pigment in a fresco.
Eyes embraced reflect a different pen,
Of outlines blurred, finer lines,
A fragile collage.

I dream.

I see the glassy canvas of a millpond
Two swallows duck and weave,
Inked tailfeathers painting their song on the water.
Picture this then if you will,
Tales of teased chance and serendipity, but richly drawn.

AFTER THE LANTERN

Vanya, the steppe and song runs first with you.
Vanya, breath of song, heart of rhythm.
We wait for you in the half-light,
Early from the shadows you emerge.
As a black monk, dearth in the fields of flax
At the morbid centre, eclipsing our trifold tryst.
Deep, worthy shadow, cast with poignancy.
From the play, lit brightly comes...
Sonia.
From an unearthly garden,
Bringing life,
Eternal.

ON CAMP HILL

Nuthatches nesting. Wheep, Wheep, Wheep, Wheep, Wheep.
Staccato plainchant-calling to their brood.
A Blackcap flits across my path, bright and berry-headed.
Pairs of Blackbirds gamely fighting in the thicket.
O Shrine to canine Arthur! God rest his heart.

Loftily perched high in the canopy, a brooding nest box sits
Fit for nocturnal woodland Kings.
Goldfinches bubbling in the branches, bright as new buds.
In the beech forest, amazing ink veins of contorted branches are
Written monotone against the Spring sky.
A lone Gull incongruously sails overhead.

Tantalising tell-tale craftsmanship of the Woodpeckers,
Looming holes in the boxes hinting at their handiwork.
Again the Nuthatch calls, a driving, gibbon-like
Whooping in contralto, a measured recitative to follow.
A lone Treecreeper spirals its branch in counterpoint to
Garrulous pinking Chaffinches and gnawing Crows.

As the sun breaks in the walled garden,
Woodpeckers' automatic weapon-fire in a distant valley
Made military in the marching caws of Magpie and Rook.
A Blackbird hops across the pelouse of a parade ground.
A Robin's jerkin, fit for the King's Regiment,
His keen song the rallying call of the bugle boy.

Up in the branches a pair of majestic Mistle Thrushes
Lugubriously hop from perch to perch.
At last the loud rattle gives the game away,
And Spotted Woodpecker crowns this day.

GREENLAND

A Minotaur loiters in the car park;
startled, the grey heron idly flaps his wings and
bonfires smoulder in the distant land of Speke.

Shrouds rise from the long barrow,
neatly demarcated by a centre circle, whilst
steel ribbons of water cut the swath
contiguous to the Cambrian Hills.

'Here Be Druids' runs the sign,
ring roads double as a ley line.
A reiver's landscape.

As drifting jasmine skeins the bare trees
and full-throated thrush, shrill-weeps
stirred by the cloven boots of Pan,
I glimpse Parnassus.

Entablature cradled by dock and elder,
columns dandled and dropped by giants,
pediments kissed in briar and buckthorn.
Heraclitean labours not fit for the forecourt,
strange heresy of the Sunday-leaguers;
I can look at you ye mighty, and despair.

EVENSONG

Most disparate nation.
By turn, gracious yet ill-mannered,
Land of clipped privet and wild gorse,
        peopled with such variety.
Seamed as the rich geology of Smith
Whose striations have shaped our cities,
Voiced our hands.

Streets of market towns are pierced with
        the colours of Hogarth,
Bruegel lives in our border villages,
Bosch in the debating chamber.
Our terraces shake still to hymns old and new,
        red, or blue.

For all our Orwellian crudeness
I see the layers stretching back through time,
Uncovered by the miner,
        sweetly shaped by the mason.
I see the jewels of Albion,
Cathedrals cupped in quiet hills
Asail in the Fens, minstered in the Wolds.

From our light, angelic hills comes
        a great glory,
Polyphony in stone matched in music.
From the quiet diligence of the Tudors,
Sober introspection of a College chapel.
Well tempered dialogue,
Poising plainchant with treble, triumphant.

Softly voiced in the Anthem,
Alternating light and dark,
Tuned to the breath of God;
Boys mouth gilded words.

For us. A freely given cycle of daily devotion,
O privilege, for green-berthed
Ships of stone and song.

CHROMATOGRAPHY

First flush, childe green
Bounded by, chill grey
Dappled then, blown glass
Pregnant with, frail emerald
Cut twice, white sun
Touched always, spring light
Second flush, flocked pink
Fresh blushed, hawthorn crown
Clear palette, yellow flecked
May morning, well blossomed
Thrush voicing, choir yearning
Nature answers, spring painting

TWO CROWS FIGHTING

Willow in hand, would I sketch furiously.
To trap the glossied inkness,
the Devilled movements of claw and wing.
Pencil grains the paper
with speed, grabbing the ridges
in a satisfying clump, clump, clump..
Black feathers flurry, as smoke.
Catch up! Capture the cawing,
capture the stabbing beaks,
the strangely silent, purposeful
murdering of crows.
As charcoal on slate, so too
black wings smudge stone.
Blurred, fanning and fluttering
of pencil.
Charcoaled, driven, oneness
of crow.
Awake! Now. Clap hands, clap, clap.
The pen lifts momentarily from its course;
paper swells and rests.
Instinct replaces intent,
Daggered embrace is lost
and with indifferent air
two crows fly off - somewhere.

COPPER BEECH

Dullard that I am,
Twelve thousand times have I
Passed you
Ignorant of thee.
Diffident, not deferent.
Twelve thousand days have you
Outlived me.
Stretched your arms,
Uncurled your copper fingers,
Heaved your chest ever outwards,
Given shade and sustenance.
Unfurled your beauty, freely.
Oaken tons of fixed light,
Most generous, humbling leviathan.
Mea culpa, o lignum vitae.

THE MIDNIGHT WATCH

Face prone, neck skewed, a drowned man
I lie, awake.
Asleep - still a distant land.
And with gravelled breath, my waves boom and crash
to fill the silenced room.
Chest ebbs and flows to a diurnal beat,
lungs draw the feathered air
lunar-like in the pitch and cloistered bedspread.
Fearing a coming oneness of atom and ocean,
I am at once patient, and doctor,
One gazing, yet closely observed.
Now the coffered ceiling creeps downwards
with smothering inevitability,
waves of sleep elusive still...
But the weathered boulder in my breast
thunders on with sonorous uncertainty.
And for me with fitful fright
to lie, as a shaking Canute
To will each rolling roar
beyond the ninth wave
and reach that slumbered shore.

FALLEN DOVE

Fluttering, white-winged Ariel,
Ark-born envoy and herald of peace,
Fit to play cooing love-token or
Sanctified Spirit.
Most blesséd creature, generous bird.
Broad-naped chattel yoked freely to
Hope or oblation.

In tethered clouds we free you
And scumbled glazes we trap your aura.
White gauze or stained light,
The final dot for your beady eye,
Ascending voices, porcelain paste,
Such are tools fit to fashion your crown.

Chisel-hewn, with oak-gouged eye
Bloated heartwood, phloem-bound,
Fixed high in the holm oak,
Heavy-laden for twelve years pined.

As we are fallen, so too you have been felled.
With beak broken, your wonder-wings clipped,
No more the low bassoon captured in time.
Yet splintered as you are, how fitting
Your soul flies singing, skywards
And the trees resound with the choirs of Spring.